Frank O. Gehry

Winton Guest House
Schnabel Residence

Residential Masterpieces 18
Frank O. Gehry
Winton Guest House
Schnabel Residence

Text and Edited by Yoshio Futagawa
Photographed by Yukio Futagawa
Art direction: Gan Hosoya

Printed and bound in Japan

ISBN 978-4-87140-643-7 C1352

Frank O. Gehry
Winton Guest House
Wayzata, Minnesota, U.S.A., 1983-87
Schnabel Residence
Brentwood, California, U.S.A., 1986-89

Text by Yoshio Futagawa

Photographed by Yukio Futagawa

世界現代住宅全集18

フランク・O・ゲーリー

ウィントン・ゲストハウス　1983-87

アメリカ合衆国，ミネソタ州，ウェイサタ

シュナーベル邸　1986-89

アメリカ合衆国，カリフォルニア州，ブレントウッド

文・編集：二川由夫

企画・撮影：二川幸夫

1980年代の二つの住宅について──二川由夫
Two Residences of the 1980's *by Yoshio Futagawa*

フランク・ゲーリーは20世紀後半から世界の建築界のトップランナーであり，現代における数少ない「巨匠建築家」であるのは疑いのないことである。

カナダ，トロント生まれ，アメリカの西海岸，ロサンゼルスを拠点に60年代からそのキャリアをスタートさせた。ゲーリーは次第にカリフォルニアの建築界における中心的人物となったが，70年代までは，アメリカ国内の東西海岸に起こる対比的な建築ムーブメントの一方の雄としての国内ローカルな存在であった。

彼を世界的に有名にすることとなった最初のマスターピースは，サンタモニカの住宅地に建つ小さな自邸であった。1978年，この小さな住宅の改築で見せた斬新な形態とマテリアルの操作は，彼の生み出した個人的な方法論の結晶ではあったが，当時の建築界にあった末期的なモダニズムの収束感や，それに取って代わろうとするポストモダニズムの言語操作の不自由な状況を吹き飛ばすのに十分な，エポック・メイキングな事件となった。

ゲーリーはこの自邸での評価以後，さらなる快進撃を続けていくことになる。ロサンゼルスの「ウォルト・ディズニー・コンサートホール」(1987-2003年)，スペインの「ビルバオ・グッゲンハイム美術館」(1991-97年) など，大スケールの公共建築の大成功によってその地位を不動のものにし，その仕事は世界各地に広がっていった。彼のつくり出す作品は，その独自な建築的，そして彼にしかつくることのできない芸術的な価値とともに，親しみやすいシルエットが奏でるシンボル性が一般人の感性にも直ぐに受け入れられた。それゆえその建築は地域のイコンとなり，多大な経済効果を生み出すこととなる。これらの成功はゲーリーを従来の建築家らしからぬ，カルチャースターとしての有名人に押し上げることになった。この時点では，ゲーリーとその作品群は現代の速い消費構造の中に取り込まれて，単なるファッションとして消えていくかにも思える勢いであった。しかし，消えるどころか，世紀を跨ぎ，彼は依然としてトップシーンに君臨している。彼の建築家を超えた高い作家性は，他に並ぶものの無い独特でパーソナルなものである。

ゲーリーの事務所が今も昔も変わらないことは，スタディに使われる大小様々な模型の量であろう。実際の材料で組み立てられたリアルな１分の１のモックアップからプロジェクトの初期につくられる小さな積み木のようなダイアグラムの模型まで，そして様々なプロダクトデザインの試作からレディ・ガガのためにデザインされた帽子のモックアップまで，巨大なスタジオ内は模型によって埋め尽くされている。模型は様々なスケールの大きさ，素材，ディテールの与えられ方で，プロジェクトの進行中につくられ，常にデザイン・デヴェロップメントの要である。模型での検証結果は，３次元ディジタイザでCADプロ

Frank Gehry was a world-class leading figure in the domain of architecture in the late 20th century, and is no doubt one of the few 'master architects' of the contemporary age.

Born in Toronto, Canada, he started his career in the 60s, based in Los Angeles on the American West Coast. Gehry gradually became a pillar of the architecture world in California, but until the 70s his presence was local and limited within the US, as the best in the West of the two contrasting architectural movements taking place on the Eastern and Western coasts of the US.

His first masterpiece that propelled him to world fame was his own residence, a small house built in a residential area in Santa Monica. In 1978, the innovative form and materials manipulation shown in the renovation of this small house was the embodiment of personal methods that he developed on his own, that eventually became a phenomenon epoch-making enough to blow away the feeling of conclusion of Modernism's terminal phase and the lack of freedom in the language manipulation of Post Modernism, the upcoming successor, that prevailed in the world of architecture of the time.

After gaining a reputation with this residence, he continued on with his success. The huge triumphs achieved through large-scaled public architectures such as the Walt Disney Concert Hall (1987-2003) in Los Angeles and the Guggenheim Museum Bilbao in Spain (1991-97) firmly established his status and his works began to spread around the world. His creations, their architectural and artistic values that are unique to him, as well as symbolic values generated by their friendly silhouettes were immediately accepted by the public sensibility. As a consequence, these architectures became the local icons, producing major economical effects. Such success pushed Gehry to notoriety as a cultural star, an unconventional status for an architect. At the time it looked as if Gehry and his works were riding a surge of momentum that would eventually swallow them into the fast contemporary consumption structure and simply go out of fashion. But in reality, instead of fading away, he is still reigning at the top as we enter the new millennium. His brilliant artistry that transcends the field of architecture is unparalleled, truly unique and personal.

One thing that never changes in Gehry's studio is the tremendous amount of study models of various sizes. From detailed 1/1 mockups using real materials to small models of wooden block-like diagrams created at a project's early phase, or from prototypes of diverse product designs to the mockup of Lady Gaga's hat, the huge studio is filled with models. Models made with different scales and sizes, materials and details during the progress of the project are at all times the key component of design development. Result data verified by models are put into CAD programs via 3D digitizers. Design is refined using computers, from which new study models are gener-

グラムに入力され，コンピュータ上でデザインのリファインが行われ，そこから再び新たなスタディ模型がつくられるといった具合に，デジタルとアナログの世界の往復が繰り返されている。

　ゲーリーの手法で常に気づかされることは，一見建築的な規範から逸脱してアヴァンギャルドに見えるものの，実は非常にオーソドックスな建築デザインのプロセスに誠実に則っていることである。にもかかわらずアウトプットの新しさは常に驚くべきものである。

　ゲーリーは大スケールの公共建築を手がける以前，自邸をはじめ10数軒の個人住宅を実現させている。それぞれの住宅はプログラムもコンテクストも異なるものであるが，ゲーリーの建築哲学の結晶であり，それぞれに固有のユニークネスを持っている。現在のゲーリー事務所のプロダクション・プロセスで用いられる最新のデジタル・テクノロジーとは異なる，模型の採寸と手書き図面，すべて手作業によるデザイン・デヴェロップメントによって生み出された小品たちは，手の痕跡の残る温かみのあるものであり，今なおその輝きを失ってはいない。

「ウィントン・ゲストハウス」
アート・コレクターであるウィントン夫妻に依頼されたこのゲストハウスは，ミネアポリスから30マイルほど離れたミネトンカ湖岸沿いの豊かな緑に囲まれた敷地に建っていた（後年，移築されている）。施主

夫妻は，50年代にフィリップ・ジョンソンに設計を依頼した主屋に長く住んでいたが，孫たちやゲストを泊めるためのゲストハウスを求め，ゲーリーに設計を依頼した。豊かな自然の広がる敷地を分割することなく，ジョンソン設計の端正なモダニズム建築と共存する小建築の要請に，ゲーリーはゲストハウスを住宅建築というより大きな屋外彫刻として実現している。この彫刻建築は主屋と対比的に配置されるものの，モダニズム建築と「アーキ・スカルプチュア」としてのある種の協調関係を生み出している。

　建物は六つの異なる大きさ，形態，素材，色彩の与えられたヴォリュームが寄り添う形で構成されている。これらのつくり出す群としてのシルエットは，画家ジョルジョ・モランディの静物画に影響されたという絶妙のバランスを保っている。2次元の静物画が完璧なバランスを保つこととは異なり，3次元のゲストハウスは，母屋からの眺めは勿論のこと，360度すべてのアングルからの眺めが刻々と変化し，見る者を飽きさせない。それぞれにプログラムを与えられたヴォリュームは隙間を与えられ，ゲストハウスを構成するエレメントとして分節されていることを表明するとともに，それぞれの形態の完結性を暗示している。また，ゲストハウスとしての非日常性を形態が表現したユーモラスで楽しげなものとなっている。

　中央に配置された天に向かってそびえ建つピラミッド型のヴォリュ

ated. There is a constant to and from between digital and analog worlds.

What stands out in Gehry's method is that, although looking avant-gardist and seemingly deviant from the norms of architecture, they are in reality faithfully based on extremely orthodox architectural design process. And yet the output is always novel and surprising.

Before his venture into large-scaled public architectures, Gehry has built more than a dozen private residences including his own. The houses differ from one another in terms of program and context, but are all fruits of Gehry's architectural philosophy, each with its own particularity and uniqueness. These small pieces of works created through entirely manual design development, hand-written drawings and model measurements that are totally different from the latest technology used in the design process at Gehry's studio today, all retain the warmth of human hands and have lost none of their luster.

Winton Guest House
Commissioned by the Wintons, an art collector couple, this guest house stood on a site surrounded by the lush greenery of Lake Minnetonka some 30 miles from Minneapolis (and was later relocated). Having lived for a long time in the main house designed by Philip Johnson in the 50s, the client couple asked Gehry to design a guest house for their grandchildren and

guests. Their request for a small architecture that would coexist with the clean-cut Modernist architecture by Johnson without having to divide the property full of natural character was realized by Gehry as a huge outdoor sculpture rather than a residential architecture. Although positioned contrastingly with regard to the main house, this sculptural architecture forges a certain type of partnership with the Modernist architecture as an 'archisculpture.'

The building consists of six volumes of different size, form, material and hues nestled together. The silhouette of this cluster of volumes maintains an exquisite balance that was inspired by the still-life studies by the painter Giorgio Morandi. Unlike the two-dimensional still-life that stays in perfect balance, the three-dimensional guest house offers ever-changing views from the main house as well as all 360 degrees around that is ever delightful to the eye. Each volume is given a specific program and arranged with a gap in between, both expressing the segmentation of elements that make up the guest house and suggesting the independence of each form. There is also a sense of fun and humor as the forms express the out-of-the-ordinary nature of a guest house.

Rising up to the sky in the center, the pyramid-shaped volume is the focus of the elements that constitute the guest house, accommodating the living and dining spaces. Its exterior is clad in painted metal sheets and has a highly abstract

ームは，ゲストハウスを構成するエレメントをまとめる焦点であり，リビングとダイニング・スペースを収めている。外装はペイントされたメタルシートで葺かれ，抽象性の高いフォルムを持つが，その内部はニュートラルな白い空間で，高い天井と空の青と周囲の木立の緑を切り取る天窓群に彩られたカジュアルで開放的な空間となっている。長い箱型のヴォリュームは小さなキッチンとガレージなどのサービス機能を収容し，外装は合板による。このヴォリュームの上には亜鉛メッキ・パネルで被覆されたスリーピング・ロフトであるボックスが，つっかえ棒のような円柱に支えられてはみ出すようにカジュアルに置かれている。煉瓦に覆われ，頂部に煙突が突き出たヴォリュームの内部は暖炉のあるアルコーブであり，リビングルームに向けて開かれている。二つの寝室はそれぞれ浴室を備え，一つは表現的なカーブが与えられ，外壁がミネソタ産のカソタ・ストーンで覆われており，もう一方は片流れ屋根を持ち，メタルシートで被覆されている。

内部の諸室はカジュアルで流動的な動線で統合的に結ばれて一軒の家を形成している。それぞれの空間には外部を窺うことができるさまざまな開口が与えられ，常に外に広がる景色を楽しむことができる。

「シュナーベル邸」
施主の夫妻は元駐フィンランド大使の夫と，建築を勉強し，ゲーリー

の事務所で働いた経験を持つ夫人であり，その設計プロセスにも積極的に参加した。「シュナーベル邸」はゲーリーの手がけた個人住宅の中でも大型のもので，その構成は集落的であり，分節される多様な形態にはそれぞれに明快なアイデンティティが与えられることで，豊かな風景がつくられると同時に，その内部の空間の豊かさは空間的，機能的に連鎖している。それぞれの棟は単体の独立した存在として美学的に成立するとともに，総体として一つの建物群がつくり出す絶妙な均衡の風景となっている。

ロサンゼルスの閑静な住宅街，ブレントウッド・ヒルズの一画の敷地は西側の前面道路から伸びる東西に細長い形状で，長手に沿って高低差があり，庭は二つのレベルに分割されている。上レベルの庭を道路よりアプローチすると，左右にガレージとゲストルーム棟を見ながら，正面奥にある主屋の玄関へ進んで行くことになる。

敷地の上レベル主屋より南西側のゲストルーム棟は，スタッコ仕上げでその頂部を飾るドームは銅板が被覆されるが，これはロサンゼルスの名所であるグリフィス天文台にインスパイアされたものである。その南側，敷地境界線に沿ってラップ・プールが配置されている。

上レベル北西側，スタッコ仕上げのガレージを収めるヴォリュームの上には，スタッフの住居である方形のヴォリュームが向きをずらされて積み重ねられている。このガレージから銅板に被覆されたアーケ

form, while its interior holds a neutral, white space with a casual and open feeling adorned with a series of skylights that frame the green of the surrounding trees, the blue of the sky and the ceiling height. The rectangular box-shaped volume houses service facilities including a kitchenette and garage, its exterior covered in plywood. On top of this volume, a box housing the sleeping loft clad in galvanized metal panels is casually placed slightly off the edge, supported on a prop-like column. Inside the brick-covered volume with a chimney sticking out from the top is an alcove with a fireplace that is open toward the living room. The two bedrooms have private bathrooms: one is given an expressive curve and exterior walls covered with Kasota stone of Minnesota origin, while the other is shed-roofed and clad in metal sheathing.

The interior of each room is integrally connected by easy, fluid lines of circulation to form a house. Each space features a variety of openings with outdoor views to enjoy the expansive landscape.

Schnabel Residence
The client couple, a former ambassador to Finland and his wife who has studied architecture and once worked at Gehry's studio, took an active part in the design process. The Schnabel Residence is a larger example of private houses designed by Gehry. Its village-like composition encloses diverse seg-

mented forms that are each given specific identities to create a colorful scenery, while richness of interior is linked both spatially and functionally. Each wing aesthetically stands on its own as an independent presence. The group of buildings as a whole creates a scenery of fine balance.

Located in Brentwood Hills, a quiet residential area in Los Angeles, the site is an elongated plot of land that stretches from the front street on the west side, with an inclination along the east-west axis that divides the garden in two levels. Approaching the upper-level garden from the street, the entrance to the main house is found further in the back, past the garage and the guestroom building on left and right.

Placed on the site's upper level, the stucco-finished guest room wing on the southwestern side of the main building is topped with a sheet copper-clad dome inspired by the Griffith Observatory, a Los Angeles landmark. On the south side is a lap pool along the site's border.

On the northwestern side of the upper level is a stucco-finished volume housing the garage, with a cubic volume housing the living space for the personnel stacked with an angle. Starting from this garage, a copper-clad colonnaded arcade extends to the kitchen in the main building along the site's northern boundary.

On the southeastern side of the site's upper level is a stand-alone building accommodating the son's studio and bed-

ードの列柱が北側敷地境界線に沿って主屋のキッチンに伸びている。

　上レベル南東側には，息子のためのスタジオと寝室を収めた棟が独立して配置される。棟は銅板によって葺かれたふた山の鋸屋根が与えられている。

　主屋は十字形プランの建物でこの住宅の焦点となる。あたかも積み木のようにヴォリューム群が組み合わされた外観は，鉛が被覆された銅板で抽象的に仕上げられている。建物は西側の玄関，中央のリビングルーム，北側のダイニングルーム，南側の暖炉のアルコーブからなる。リビングルームである中央部分は３層吹き抜けであり，スカイライトからの自然光に満たされた明るい空間である。

　この十字形の建物の北側に接するように配置される２階建ての方形のヴォリュームは，１階に前述のキッチンや家族室，書斎，２階に二つの寝室を収める。外装表現をスタッコ仕上げにすることで主屋と明快に区別される。

　敷地の下レベルには水深の浅い水盤が広がる。この水庭の上に主寝室棟が浮かぶように配置される。主寝室棟は主屋同様に鉛被覆の銅板で覆われ，シンボリックなハイサイドライトが頂部に置かれる。周囲を銅板被覆の彫刻的な列柱に取り囲まれ，彫刻的な配置であるとともに機能的にプライバシーが獲得されている。水庭の西端は，浴室，ドレッシングルーム，サウナ，ジムといった主寝室のための諸室が配置

されるガラス張りのアーケードとなっている。主寝室棟は水庭に映り込む虚像によって増幅され，上レベルの庭の賑やかな風景とは対極的な精神的で静寂に包まれた風景である。その風景は水面が敏感に受容する陽光や風の移ろいに彩られ，刻々とその姿を変えてみせる。

「ウィントン・ゲストハウス」と「シュナーベル邸」に共通して見られるゲーリーの方法論は，建築的言語である窓やドアといった規格品的なエレメントや，煙突や勾配屋根などの誰もが共有している建築の記号，そこに用いられる建材や仕上げに普遍的な性格を確実に持たせると同時に，それらのスケールやプロポーション，用法を巧みに操作することで，普遍性から生まれる新しい意味を建物に付加し，ヴォリュームや形態の操作によって彫刻化され「脱建築」する事態を見事に食い止めて，彫刻的な建築を成立させていることである。

room, featuring a copper-sheathed, double saw-tooth roof.

The main house is a cross-shaped building and represents the residence's focal point. From the outside the cluster of volumes looks like a pile of wooden blocks, clad in lead-covered copper sheets. The building consists of an entrance on the west, living room in the center, dining room on the north, and an alcove with a fireplace on the south. The central core housing the living room is a bright, triple-height space filled with natural light pouring from the skylight.

The two-storied rectangular volume arranged adjacent to the north side of this cross-shaped building accommodates the aforementioned kitchen, family room, study, and two upstairs bedrooms. Exterior expression is accentuated with stucco finish that clearly distinguishes it from the main building.

On the site's lower level is the shallow expanse of water. The master bedroom, clad in lead-covered copper sheets like the main building and topped with a symbolic high side light, seems to float on this wading pool. Sculpturesque copper columns surround the master bedroom, providing privacy. Various spaces for the master bedroom such as bathroom, dressing room, sauna and gym are arranged within a glazed arcade along the western edge of the wading pool. The master bedroom wing is visually amplified by the reflection on the wading pool within a scenery of spirituality and serenity that is the opposite of the lively scenery of the upper-level garden. It

is an ever-changing scenery of passing winds and sunlight on the sensitive water surface.

One aspect of Gehry's methodology that is common to both Winton Guest House and Schnabel Residence is the successful achievement of the 'archisculpture' as he adds to the buildings new meanings that emerge from universality and skillfully holds back the 'de-architecturizing' situation through sculpturization by volume and form manipulation, by giving without fail a universal character to standardized elements such as windows and doors that make up the architectural language, to architectural symbols shared by everybody such as the chimney or the pitched roof, and to the building materials and finishes used there, as well as by adeptly manipulating their scales, proportions and using methods.

English translation by Lisa Tani

Winton Guest House 1983-87

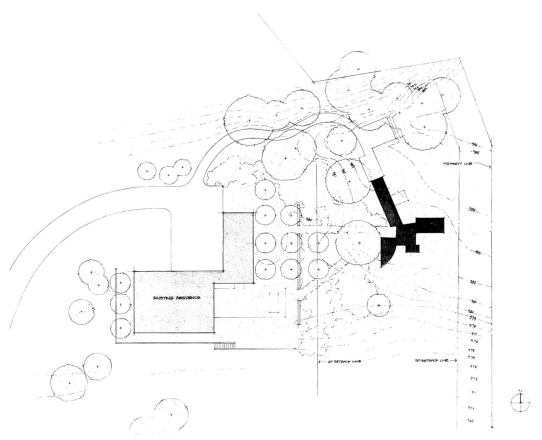

Site plan

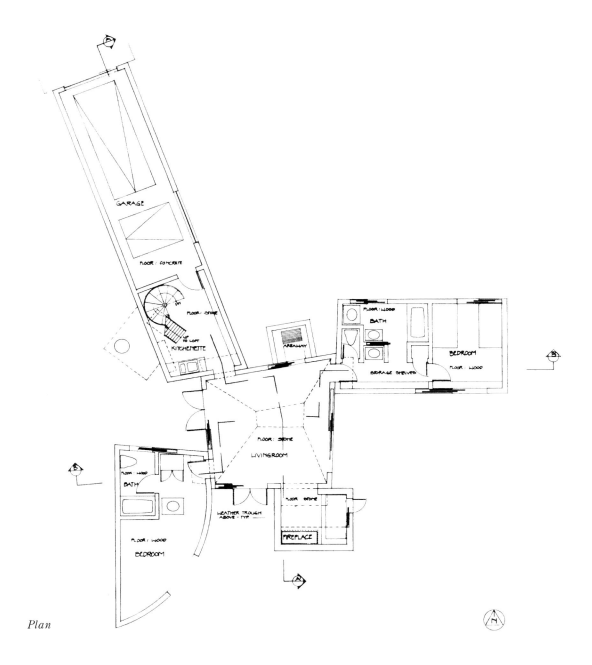

Plan

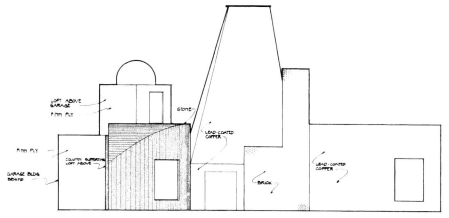

South elevation

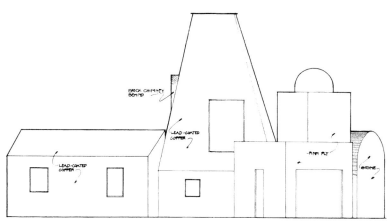

North elevation

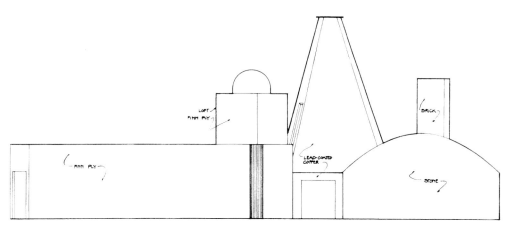

West elevation

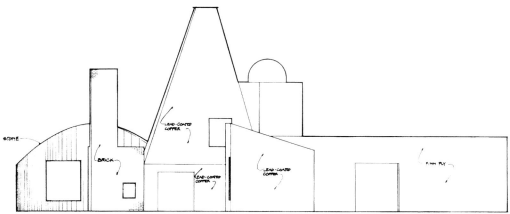

East elevation

View from southwest. Each volume has different form and finishing material

View from south

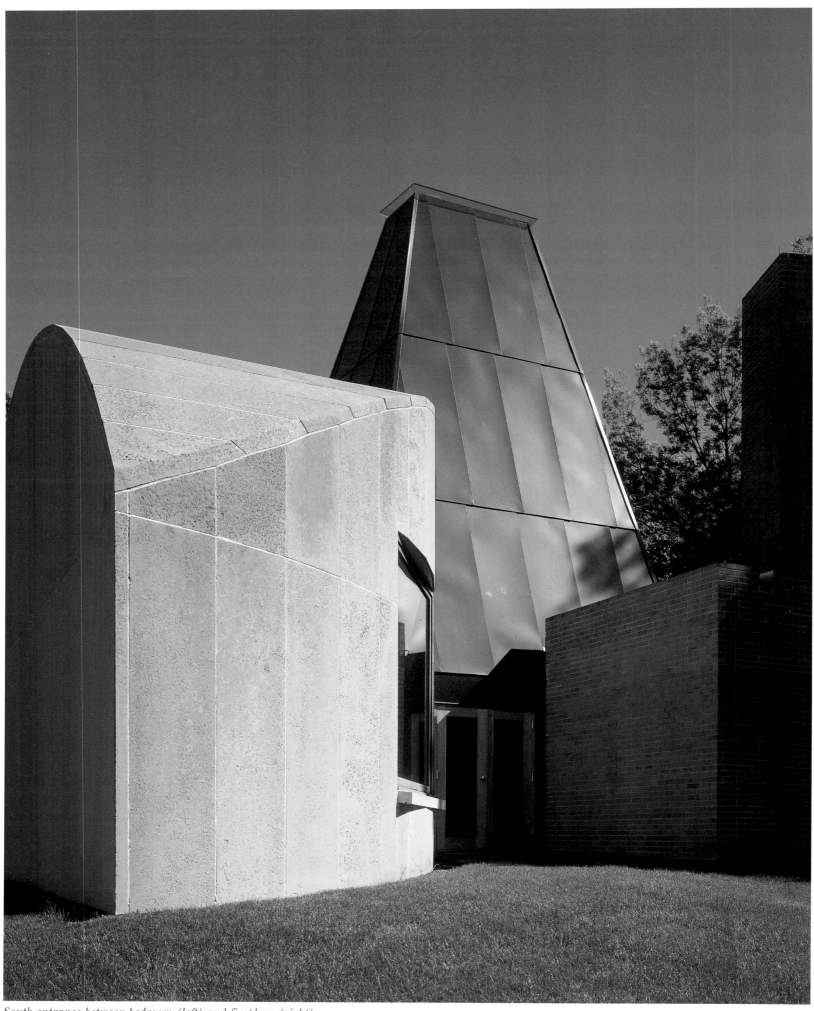

South entrance between bedroom (left) and fireplace (right)

East entrance

View from northwest

West entrance

View from west

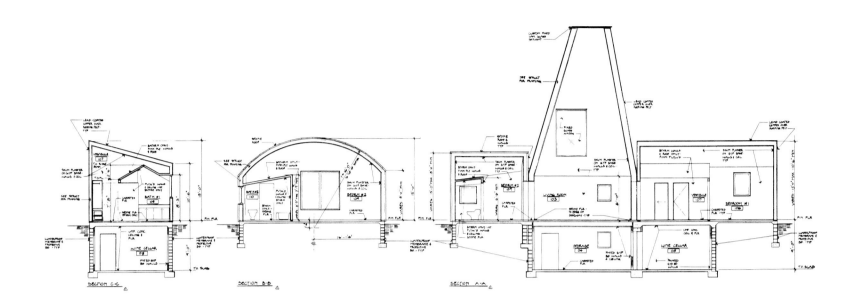

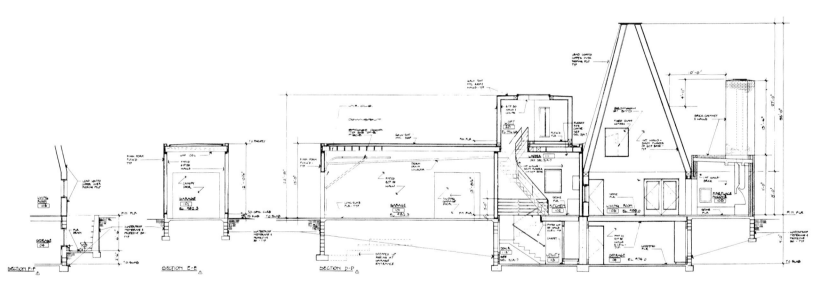

Sections

Bedroom (right) and loft (left)

Living room

Skylights of living room

Living room: south entrance (right) and fireplace alcove (left)

Fireplace alcove

Living room: view toward kitchenette

Kitchenette: staircase to loft above

Bedroom

Sketches by Frank O. Gehry

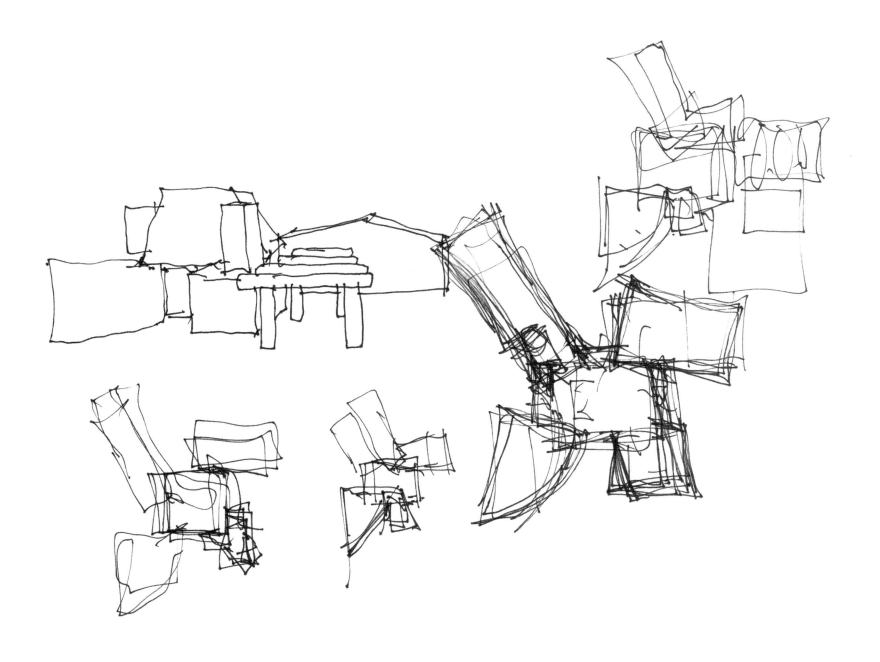

Schnabel Residence 1986-89

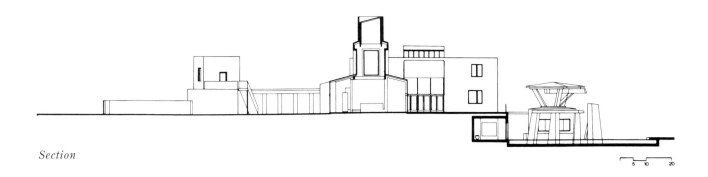

Section

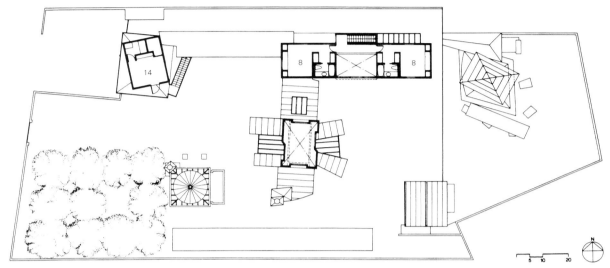

Upper level

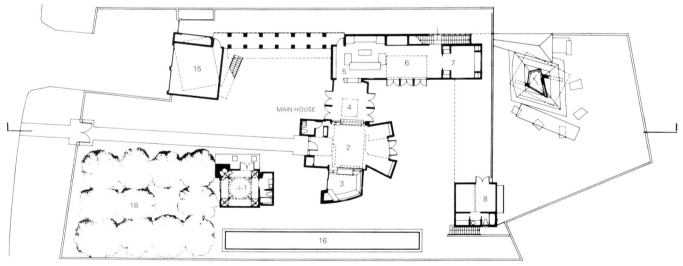

Middle level

1 GUESTHOUSE
2 LIVING ROOM
3 FIREPLACE
4 DINING ROOM
5 KITCHEN
6 FAMILY ROOM
7 STUDY
8 BEDROOM
9 MASTER BEDROOM
10 LIBRARY
11 DRESSING ROOM
12 SAUNA
13 WORKOUT
14 CARETAKER'S ROOM
15 GARAGE
16 LAP POOL
17 REFLECTING POOL
18 OLIVE GROVE

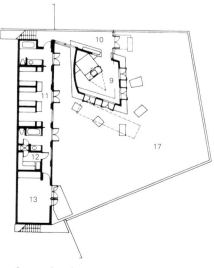

Lower level

Guesthouse on right

Main house: view from northwest

View from southeast.
Main house (right) and guesthouse (left)

Living room: looking west toward approach

Living room: looking north toward dining room

Living room: view from dining room toward fireplace

Skylights of living room

Fireplace

Kitchen

Living room: looking east toward garden

View from reflecting pool on east. Master bedroom on right

Master bedroom: view from south

Master bedroom: view from east

Downward view of master bedroom

Staircase connecting master bedroom and main house

Corridor on upper level: door of bedroom

Master bedroom

Master bedroom

Upward view of highside light

Highside light of master bedroom

BRENTWOOD RES.   GEHRY '87

Sketches by Frank O. Gehry

Photographs are taken by Yukio Futagawa except as noted below
pp.16-17, p.29, p.30, pp.34-35, pp.37-45, pp.49-58, p.61, p.62 above: photos by W.Fujii

世界現代住宅全集18
フランク・O・ゲーリー
ウィントン・ゲストハウス
シュナーベル邸

2015年4月24日発行
文・編集：二川由夫
撮影：二川幸夫
アート・ディレクション：細谷巌

印刷・製本：大日本印刷株式会社
制作・発行：エーディーエー・エディタ・トーキョー
151-0051　東京都渋谷区千駄ヶ谷3-12-14
TEL.(03)3403-1581（代）

ISBN 978-4-87140-643-7 C1352